EXPLOR
GRIEF

An Enchanté
Inner-Active Book

Written by the Enchanted Family
Illustrated by Tina Cash

Enchanté Publishing
120 Hawthorne, Palo Alto, CA 94301
1-800-473-2363

Foreword

The ability to feel is one of a child's most precious gifts. Every child is born with a deep desire to love and be loved. Underneath a child's anger, hurt, jealousy, and fear is love and a need to feel close. The people for whom children can sometimes feel the most negative emotion—parent, stepparent, sibling, teacher, friend— are those they also care most about. When it comes to feelings, no one is wrong.

Setting the stage for your child to be able to do this workbook, with optimal results, requires providing a place where the child can feel safe and have the necessary tools available for coloring and cutting. The book has been created so the child can do as much as possible on his/her own. However, you can assist by reading instructions, answering questions, and listening if your child wants to share. The Inner-Active workbooks are a unique and practical gift for children and all those who love and nurture them.

—Sirah Vettese, Ph.D., co-author of
Lifemates: The Love Fitness Program for a Lasting Relationship
—Harold H. Bloomfield, M.D., author of the best-selling
How to Survive the Loss of A Love and *How to Heal Depression*

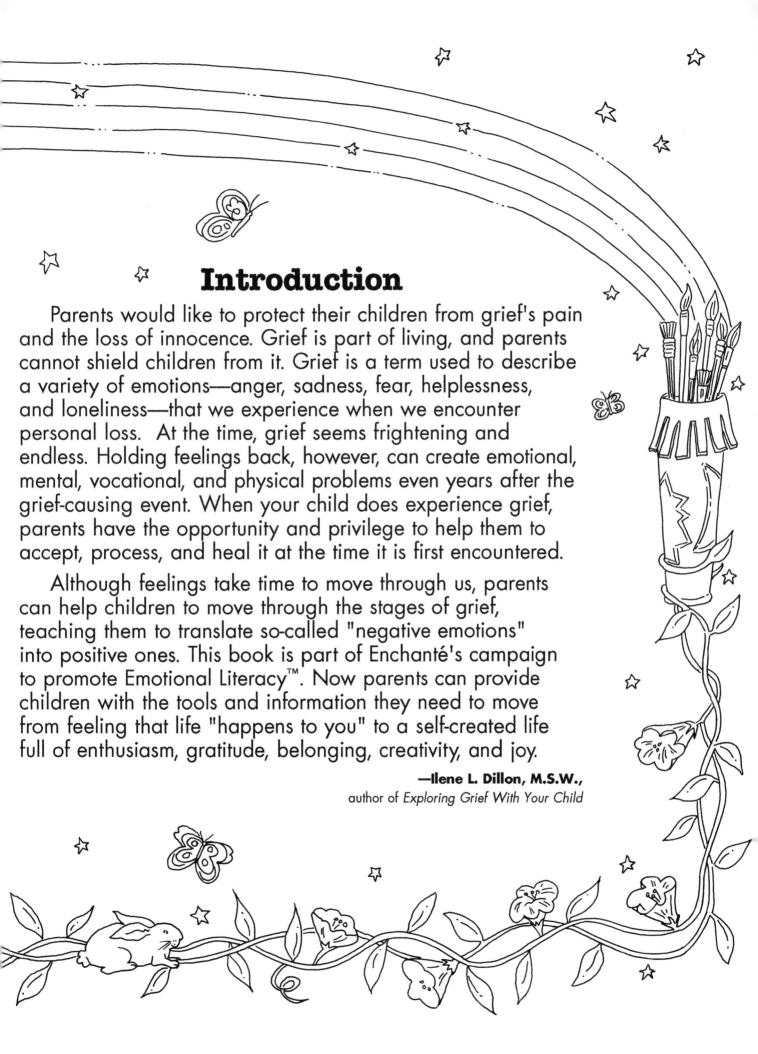

Introduction

Parents would like to protect their children from grief's pain and the loss of innocence. Grief is part of living, and parents cannot shield children from it. Grief is a term used to describe a variety of emotions—anger, sadness, fear, helplessness, and loneliness—that we experience when we encounter personal loss. At the time, grief seems frightening and endless. Holding feelings back, however, can create emotional, mental, vocational, and physical problems even years after the grief-causing event. When your child does experience grief, parents have the opportunity and privilege to help them to accept, process, and heal it at the time it is first encountered.

Although feelings take time to move through us, parents can help children to move through the stages of grief, teaching them to translate so-called "negative emotions" into positive ones. This book is part of Enchanté's campaign to promote Emotional Literacy™. Now parents can provide children with the tools and information they need to move from feeling that life "happens to you" to a self-created life full of enthusiasm, gratitude, belonging, creativity, and joy.

—Ilene L. Dillon, M.S.W.,
author of *Exploring Grief With Your Child*

What color is your sadness?
Draw a picture or design using that color.

Draw a picture of what you have lost.

Look at the pictures.
Color in the events that have happened.

My Story

Draw or write a story about an
event that has made you sad.

Find the hidden feelings as you color in
the patterns in the kaleidoscope.

1 – Yellow *(denial)*

2 – Red *(anger)*

3 – Orange *(bargaining)*

4 – Blue *(depression)*

5 – Green *(acceptance)*

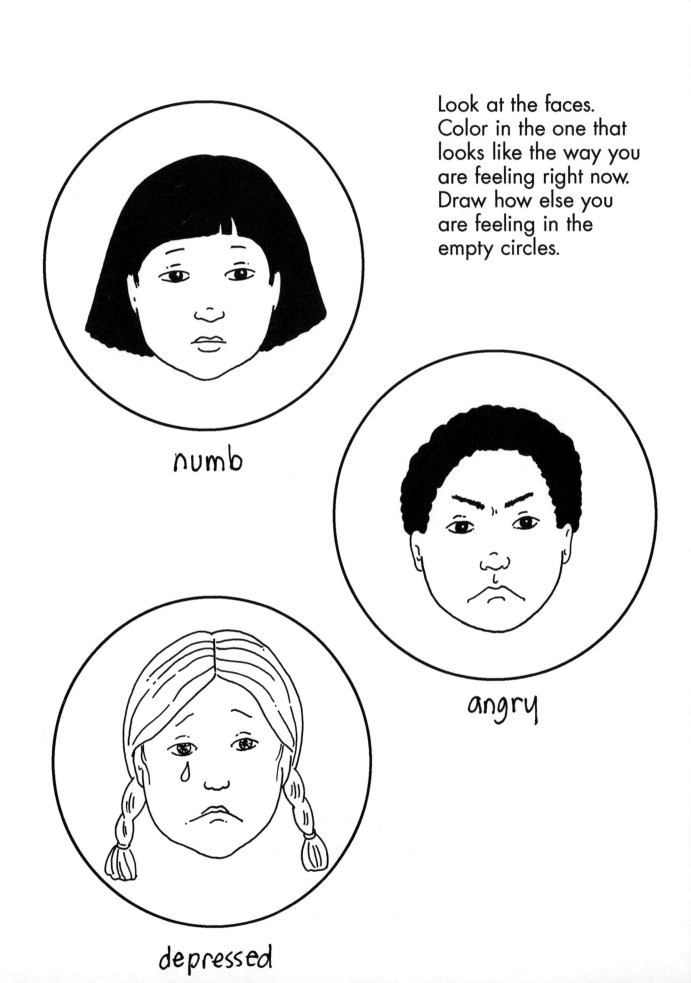

Look at the faces.
Color in the one that
looks like the way you
are feeling right now.
Draw how else you
are feeling in the
empty circles.

numb

angry

depressed

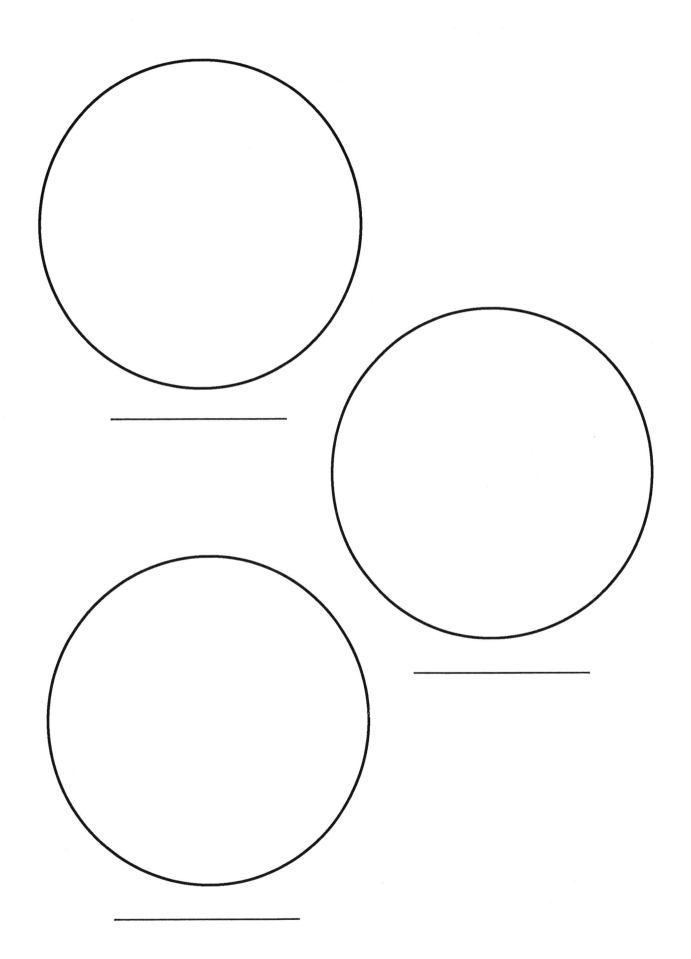

CYCLES OF LIFE

What stage is missing in each cycle?

butterfly   eggs   larva   cocoon

spring   summer   fall

seed   seedling   bloom

Draw the missing stage in each cycle.
Color in the pictures.

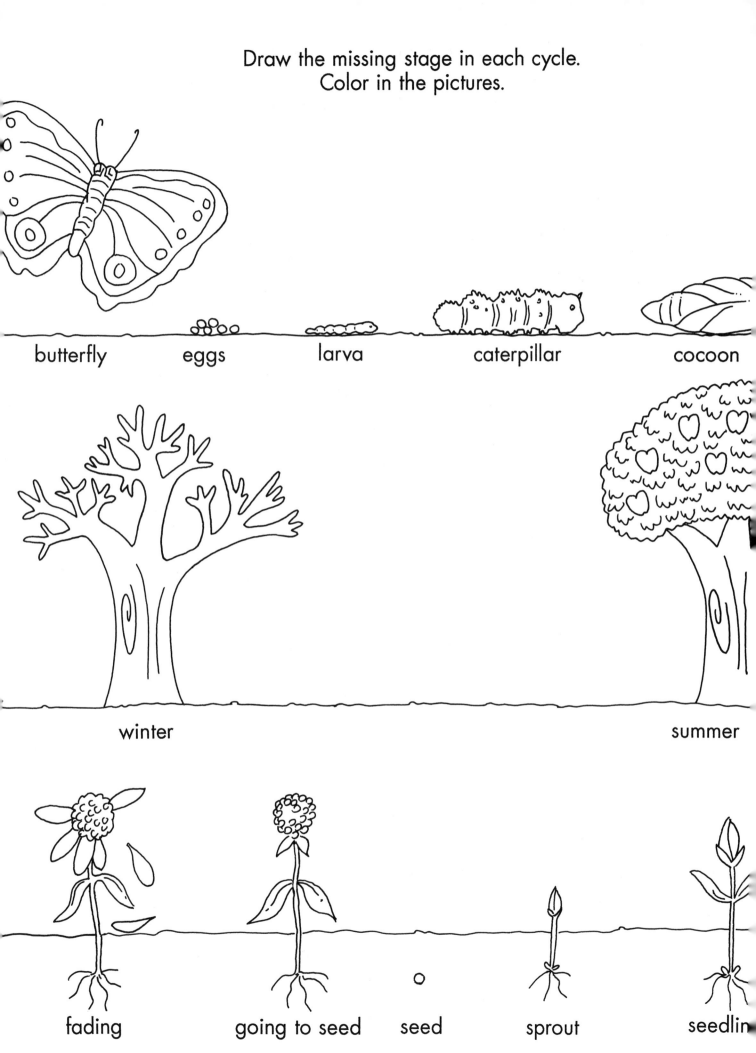

butterfly   eggs   larva   caterpillar   cocoon

winter   summer

fading   going to seed   seed   sprout   seedlin

Color in the jewels that describe what you miss
about the person or thing you have lost.
Add your own ideas in the empty jewels and hearts.

Cut and paste old magazines, postcards, flowers, or anything you wish, to create a collage in memory of what you have lost.

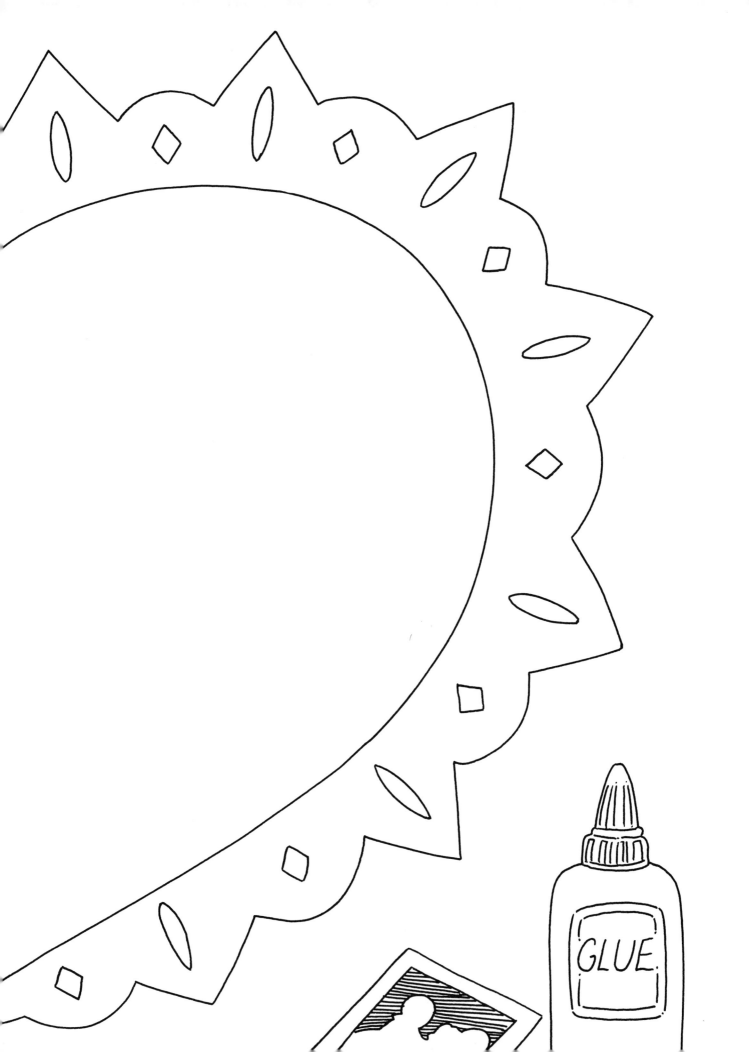

GLUE

Color in the picture as you go
through the cave to the other side.

1. Imagine you are walking
   through a dark cave. You
   have been walking for a
   long time, feeling heavy
   with sadness and grief.

2. Is there any way you can
   let go of your sadness?

3. Going toward the light
   ahead of you, you
   hear rushing water.

4. In front of you
   is a beautiful
   pond and
   waterfall.

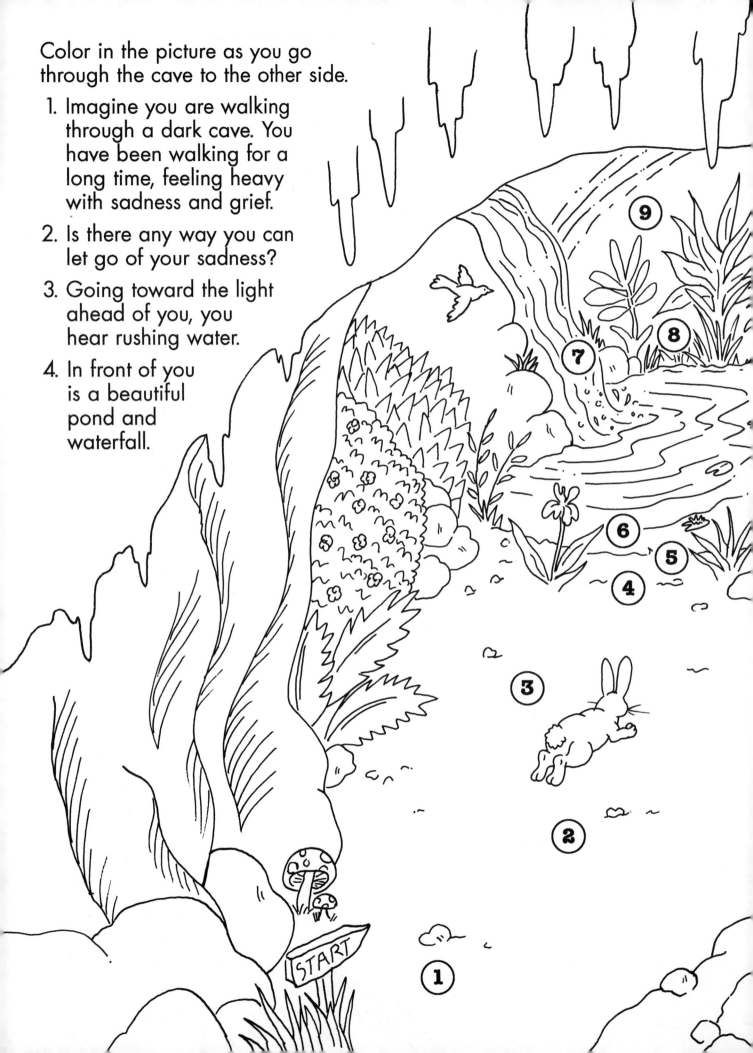

5. Above the waterfall you notice a magical rainbow.

6. You step into the pool of clear water.

7. Swim to the waterfall and stand quietly while the magic water washes away your grief and sadness.

8. Step out on the other side feeling calm and peaceful.

9. Reach out and wrap yourself in the rainbow colors.

Now that you know the path to the magical waterfall, close your eyes and imagine yourself going to that special place of peace and quiet where sadness and grief melt away.

Forgive and Let Go

PLAY MY FAVORITE MUSIC

TAKE A BUBBLE BATH

GIVE A HUG

GET A HUG

TALK TO A FRIEND

WALK TO A SPECIAL PLACE

Write the things that would make you feel better
in the hearts and draw yourself in the center.